Memories of HUDDERSFIELD

Foreword

There are those who may argue that Huddersfield essentially has hardly changed over the years. That the town clings resolutely to its image as a stolid symbol of Yorkshire values. Oh indeed, the architects and town planners may have created some remarkable and magnificent emblems of the twentieth century - The Alfred McAlpine Stadium is the most obvious example, but within the town itself the changes have been more subtle.

Nowadays, rock concerts may well be regular and welcome features of Huddersfield's tourist attractions, but the wealth of architectural splendour that has withstood the passage of time is indisputable and memorable. Saint George's Square remains virtually unchanged, although skillful craftsmanship has gone into preserving that formidable appearance.

But memorable too is the community spirit that has always been an integral part of Huddersfield life and that's created by people. People working together, playing together and just getting on with their everyday lives. Perhaps more than anything else that's what this book celebrates. If you've grown up in Huddersfield your past will be here. Gone on, wallow a little.

Alex Hall

Alex Hall, Presenter - The Alex Hall Phone-In on The Pulse of West Yorkshire

First published in March 1996.
Revised in October 1996 by:
TRUE NORTH PUBLISHING,
Dean Clough Industrial Park,
Halifax HX3 5AX. Tel (01422) 344344
Repro. by Transgraphic Ltd., Morley.
Printed by Joseph Ward Colourprint Ltd., Dewsbury.

ISBN 1 900 463 15 6

Contents

1..Leisure

2..At Work

3..Wheels of Time

4..Sporting Moments

5..Changing Face of the Town Centre

6..Outskirts

7........................ ....Bird's Eye View

8 ....Visitors, VIPs & Celebrations

Acknowledgements

Virtually all of the photographs contained within this book are from private collections. The publishers would therefore like to thank: Mr Morris Bray (Photographer) and the management of Greaves Photographers, both of Huddersfield. The quality of the photographs provided by the aforementioned was first rate and is a testament to their skill in the art of photography. In addition Mr Geoff Lumb and Mr Ian Thomas provided very welcome help by allowing the use of photographs from their substantial personal collections. We would also like to thank the advertisers within this book, many of which are local businesses and as such have played a part in the history of Huddersfield. Thanks must also go to Mr Gareth Martin for organising the advertising content.

This photograph was taken at Lindley Carnival and Gala Day in June 1953. Most neighbourhoods held annual Gala Days in the 1950s with local children enjoying the sight of carnival floats and processions. Judging by the overcoats and headscarves being worn, the weather had not been particularly favourable for Lindley's 1953 Gala.

Left: The primary class at Holmfirth Council School gather in the school garden for this 1932 class photograph. The young boy with the cheeky grin on the front row, second from the right, is Morris Bray who went on to follow his father into the photography business. This is particularly relevant because a good deal of the 1940s and 50s pictures within this book were actually taken by Morris!

Right: The Huddersfield College building in New North Road. Huddersfield New College was actually established by the amalgamation of Hillhouse Technical School and Huddersfield College at the beginning of the school year 1957-58, though for two terms the combined school continued to occupy the existing buildings at Hillhouse and in New North Road.

The "new" school building at Salendine Nook was officially opened on 26th March, 1958, by Sir Edward Boyle, Bart., Parliamentary Secretary to the Minister of Education. Pupils and staff moved in to occupation at the beginning of the following summer term.

Huddersfield New College has since developed into one of the foremost education establishments in the North, providing a substantial stream of entrants to Oxford and Cambridge universities every year.

Right: Hopkinson's was one of the several Huddersfield firms to hold an Annual Gala. This July 1960 picture shows a young entrant in the fancy dress competition. The slogan "Drink a Pinta Milk a Day" was coined by a Government advertising campaign to promote milk consumption.

Below: Crowds gather in the seating area of the open air theatre in Greenhead Park for the 1953 "Summer Entertainments". Originally entitled "Holidays at Home" a series of events have been staged every year at Greenhead Park, beginning in 1941. The attractions were intended to coincide with the Huddersfield holiday weeks, with the climax usually being a spectacular fireworks display on the evening of the last day.

A collection of children and parents in fancy dress head for Rawthorpe Children's Field Day in June 1953. The Police car on the left of the picture seems very unobtrusive compared to today's brightly coloured vehicles, but then the level of crime in the 1950s was, on the whole, lower than it is nowadays.

Left: The 7th Duke of Wellington's Regiment Bringing out the Colours (after being stored for the duration of the War). The gentlemen marching in plain clothes were probably veterans of the two Great Wars. This picture dates from 1948.

Right: Market Street in May 1953 and the Civic Parade is in full swing. The newspaper advertising bills near the traffic lights encourage readers to sample "Rommel's own Story". Even eight years after the end of the War, it was still making newspaper headlines.

Left: During the 1950s, Huddersfield boasted more than 25 separate cinemas. Although television was available as early as 1951, it would be ten years before it was generally affordable, and therefore cinemas enjoyed enormous popularity. This picture shows the frontage of the Empire Cinema on a December evening in 1953. Famous for its double seats on the back row, the Empire was showing the Ronald Reagan film "Code of the Secret Service".

Below: The frontage of the Majestic Cinema in Viaduct Street is perhaps less glamorous than the Empire in this 1962 shot. John Wayne was topping the bill in his 1961 movie, "The Comancheros".

The Ritz Cinema on Market Street was perhaps one of the most popular picture houses in Huddersfield for many years. Owned by Associated British Cinemas (ABC as it was later called), the Ritz also boasted its own restaurant and could seat over 2000. This view of the Ritz dates from Summer 1953. In later years the ABC was to be the venue for several famous visitors to Huddersfield, including Cliff Richard and The Beatles.

During the First World War, employees of Clayton & Co (Huddersfield) Ltd formed the Karrier division of St. John's Ambulance Brigade to cope with emergencies should they arise. The members of the group are shown posing in front of one of the vehicles provided by the company for transporting the wounded, often at night, from the railway stations to the various Military Hospitals in the area, the main one being the one established at Royd's Hall, Paddock.

Left: Mr. P. S. Pearson, one of the broadcast engineers at the newly opened Holme Moss Transmitting Station, checks the "apology caption" in the main control room. This was the device that was called on to transmit the message "Normal transmission will be resumed....."
Television came to Huddersfield in October 1951 when Holme Moss began broadcasting to an area containing eleven million homes in the North. BBC was the only channel available at the time but only a tiny minority of households owned a TV set in any case.

Right: The engineer in charge of Holme Moss in 1954, Mr. C. Buckle, discussing what appears to be the list of transmission details with his assistant, Mr. D. Hinchliffe. It would be several more years before TV was available to the masses but by 1962, the new "625" lines broadcasts were available and the pages of the Huddersfield Examiner were full of advertisements for televisions to rent . The TV era had begun.

The expertise gained through the manufacture of instruments, gauges and tools, created a nucleus of highly skilled personnel. This provided the company with a suitable development team to design and manufacture Dathan's own special purpose machinery for the production of gear shaper cutters.

The production of vernier gauges was phased out by 1970 and the development team were wholly engaged in the research and production of gear cutting tools. The company moved to a purpose built factory within its own landscaped grounds at Meltham in 1974. Further extensions were built in 1980 and then in 1987.

The new facitlities enabled continuous and intense development in product design, quality control and production methods. The rack type generating cutters were included to complete a full range of gear cutting tools using the shaping method.

Above and right: The unusually high proportion of women engineering workers in these two pictures points to the fact that they were taken during the Second World War when Dathan was involved in the production of Gear cutters for the War effort. Observant readers will also spy the tin hats conveniently stored under the workbenches!

Dathan Tool and Gauge Company Ltd was founded in 1924 by the father of the present directors and his partner, Frank Rushworth. Dathan was incorporated as a limited company in 1964, and the Directors now include the third generation of the Moorhouse family. The company, in its early years, manufactured jigs, fixtures and gauges, specialising in vernier reading instruments. During the war years the product range increased to include gear shaper cutters and straight bevel generating tools.

Wellfield Quarry, at Crosland Hill, was established in 1854 to satisfy the burgeoning demand for building stone created by the new capitalists of the Industrial Revolution. Most of Huddersfield's splendidly detailed Victorian buildings - including the architecturally important Railway Station - were constructed using stone from along and atop the southern escarpment of the Colne Valley, where literally dozens of quarries co-existed. The most prolific of these were concentrated around the village of Crosland Hill and stones extracted and crafted there gained a reputation for strength and durability that lasts to this day. Nowadays, however, only Johnsons remain to uphold Crosland Hill's proud quarrying tradition. Founded in 1895, Johnsons developed a stoneworking operation simply to cater for the needs of their building commissions but the potential for expansion of the stone supply trade was quickly identified. Demand was such that future growth became dependent upon the acquisition of a building stone quarry and the famous Wellfield Quarries were bought in 1927.

Huddersfield Public Library under construction, June 1938.

The business grew steadily over the next half century before being acquired in 1979 by its present owners, The Readymix-Huddersfield Group, who provided the impetus to embark upon an ambitious and continuing programme of further expansion. Wellfield has become the largest dimensioned sandstone quarry and stoneworking yard in Britain. A range of the World's most technologically advanced stoneworking machinery and the age-old skills of a team of dedicated stonemasons combine to produce a quality of workmanship that will ensure Johnsons continue to carry the banner of Huddersfield's "stone" heritage.

Cradle of the Chemicals Industry

The chemicals industry has become interwoven with the working life of Huddersfield people throughout most of the twentieth century.
The birth of what was to become one of Huddersfield's main industries can be traced back to 1830 when Mr. Read Holliday founded his company.
At the age of 21 Mr. Holliday set up in business to distil ammonia at premises in Tanfield, off Leeds Road. By 1839 his growing concern was able to move to Turnbridge, near the Huddersfield Gas Light Company on the east of the town.
By this time Read Holliday and Sons were concentrating on the distillation of Coal Tar, which at the time was considered a waste product of gas production.
Out of this so called waste came products such as ammonia, creosote, benzene and paint solvents.
When the First World War broke out urgent expansion in dyestuffs was needed to meet war time requirements. As a result British Dyes Ltd. was set up with help from the government and the substantial site now occupied by Zeneca at Leeds Road was acquired.

By 1919 British Dyes had merged with Levinstein Limited, the other major British dyestuffs company, to form the British Dyestuffs Corporation Ltd.
In 1926 this company had become ICI, a name that was to become synonymous with Huddersfield.
By the mid 1950s the ICI works in Huddersfield was the largest employer in the area, with over 5000 staff and hundreds of contractors based at the Leeds Road site.
Some of the products that the Huddersfield ICI works have produced over the years have become household brand names, including Nylon and Terylene.

Above: An early view of the ICI works

Right: The Main Avenue at the ICI works, circa. 1948. The area to the right of the picture is where the main offices were constructed and opened in 1951. The rows of buildings were christened MacAlpine sheds after the company that constructed them. Some have survived and are still in place today.

Both pictures courtesy of Zeneca, Huddersfield Works.

Thomas Broadbent and Sons Ltd - a pioneer of engineering excellence.

The name of Broadbents is known the world over as a manufacturer of industrial centrifuges, but to Huddersfield folk the company is better known as a local employer in the engineering industry with a history going back over 130 years in the town.

The Broadbent story begins in 1864 when Thomas Broadbent set up a business as an engineer and millwright. Aged just 31, he quickly established a reputation both for the work done by his firm and his interest in the Mechanics Institute, which later became Huddersfield College of Technology, evolving into today's Huddersfield Technical College.

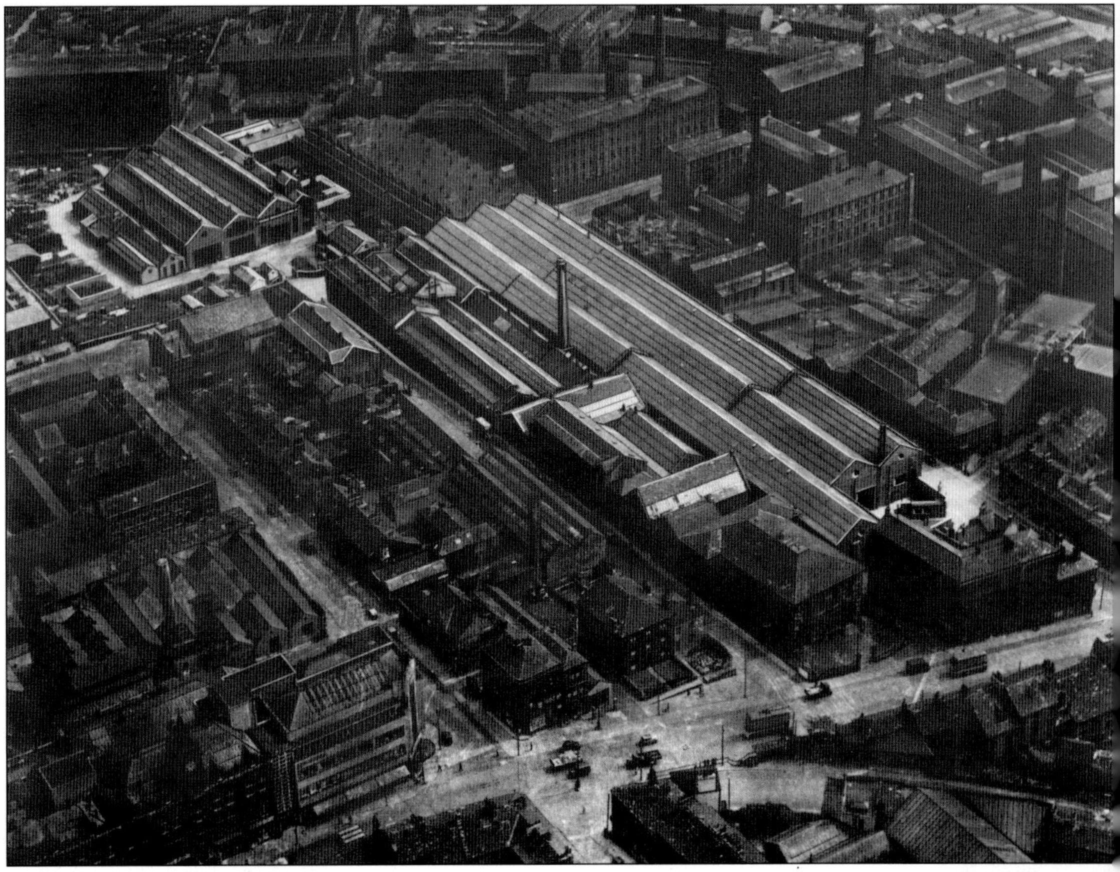

In 1870 Thomas Broadbent made his first centrifugal extractor for the extraction of water from washed wool and cloth. The many mills that made up Huddersfield's buoyant textile industry at the time found this machine to be so effective that they were soon clamouring for delivery. The business began to prosper but in 1880, at the age of 47, Thomas Broadbent died, leaving his wife, Helen and seven children. The eldest was William, then aged 16. Thomas's will decreed that the business should be sold, with the proceeds going to his widow, but this was unacceptable to Helen, as she wanted the business for her sons. She borrowed money from every possible source to enable her to retain control and despite the fact that she had seven children, she personally ran the business for five years until her two eldest sons were old enough to take on some of the responsibility.

In 1874 Thomas Broadbent built the first of a series of large steam engines for use in local textile mills. These were mostly slow running, tandem compound engines with outputs of up to 250 horsepower. The quality of workmanship and longevity of these magnificent machines ensured that several of them were still in working order up to 65 years after they were built. The engines were often given names which were usually taken from the owner's eldest daughter. Broadbent's own engine was christened Annie.

Broadbent's also diversified into motor car production for a brief period at the beginning of this century, when they produced three prototype cars. Using a six-and-a-half horsepower Astor engine, the Broadbent cars were amongst the first to be registered in Huddersfield and thus carry the local "CX" registration letters. The fact that Broadbents were able to take on such diverse manufacturing projects as motor cars and centrifuges is testament to the variety of skill possessed by the firm's workforce at the time.

Facing page, top left: An interior picture of Broadbent's works in the 1940s. ***Facing page, right:*** Broadbents premises dominates this late 1930s aerial view, which also includes the Huddersfield Co-Op building of 1936.
Left: One of the mill steam engines built by Broadbents, this one was christened "Doris". ***Above:*** The Broadbent Car, one of three built by the company in the early 1900s.

Due to the large size of the castings which were being made in the Broadbents foundry in the late 1890s, an overhead travelling crane was considered essential. No overhead cranes were made in Britain in 1892, so Broadbent's made their own. One of the first incorporated an electric motor drive which is now considered to have been the first electrically driven overhead travelling crane in the world. The crane shown on the left was only taken out of service in 1960, and in its early years was used to demonstrate the abilities of this type of crane. Over 2000 were subsequently made, an amazing quantity bearing in mind the scale of these collosal machines.

During the early 1930s bridge operating and control gear became a speciality of the company. Broadbents operating gear was subsequently installed in many out-of-the-way places, including the Bangkok Memorial Bridge, opened in 1932. Nearer to home, the famous Transporter Bridge over the Tees in Middlesborough was equipped with Broadbents operating gear. This bridge is the heaviest vertical lift type in the world, and is still in use today, providing ample evidence of the quality of Broadbents engineering.

Above: The sheer size of this Broadbent built overhead travelling crane can be seen in this picture, taken shortly after the turn of the century.
Right: The lifting gear for the famous Tees (Newport) Bridge in Middlesborough was made by Broadbents. Work began on the bridge in 1932. The combined weight of the lifting span and counter weights is 5400 tons.

Above: This photograph would have been an official secret during the war years, when Broadbents built four of these "X craft" midget submarines in conditions of total secrecy
Above right: Laundry girls at the Shirley Laundry in Southampton docks using Broadbents centrifuges in 1938.

During the First World War Broadbents came under government control, producing overhead cranes, steelworks plant and centrifuges for the war effort. The Second World War saw Broadbents make practically all the centrifuges used by the Allies in the manufacture of guncotton, as well as many other wartime components such as anti-tank guns, mortars and tank parts. Perhaps the most intriguing of all though, was the commission to build four complete "X" craft midget submarines. These were destined to play a major part in the war effort and their crews were decorated with four Victoria Cross medals, and a great many other awards. Three of Broadbents own staff were awarded the British Empire Medal for their work in overcoming the many production difficulties involved

Today, The Broadbent Group employs around 270 people and exports over half of its output. The company is still a world market leader in the manufacture of centrifuges for industries as varied as chemical and pharmaceutical, sugar production and industrial effluent treatment, with agencies in over 100 countries. But Broadbents is still based in Huddersfield and is proud to retain its local roots in the town where it all started.

BROADBENT

Ernest Brook, how one man's vision led from a Huddersfield back street to an international company.

In our modern world many wonderful inventions that we now take for granted had a sceptical reception in their early days, and their eventual development was often the result of the sheer determination of one or two men.

The alternating current electric motor is one such case in point, and the man who more than anyone else was responsible for elevating this device to the present role of the power behind modern industry was Ernest Brook, and the following three pages describe the story of how he created an international business with nothing more than an idea and the will to succeed.

Not long after the turn of the century Ernest Brook, who was then a thirty-one year old manager and designer at a local electrical engineers, decided to set up his own business to make and sell alternating current electric motors.

Up to this point Ernest Brook had carved out a somewhat chequered career, including leaving school at eleven, followed by two years at sea on a North Sea trawler, then three years as a printers apprentice, finally entering the electrical trade first in Leeds, then Stoke-on-Trent, and Cardiff before coming to Huddersfield in his late twenties.

His decision to begin his own business was driven by his belief in the future of the alternating current (AC) motor, a belief that was not shared by many other people in the electrical trade at the time. In his own time he had designed single phase motors for operation on the Huddersfield supply, at that time being 100 cycles single phase. Ernest Brook was not a rich man, so it was with virtually no capital that he set up his fledgling business in 1904. His modest means meant that his first premises were a small room in a building on Huddersfield's Threadneedle Street.

Above: Ernest Brook poses next to Brook motor number one, bought back from his first customer thirty odd years after he had supplied it. ***Left:*** Ernest Brook had an innovative approach to advertising. in the 30s Brook Motors took out a full page advert on page one of the Daily Mail. The British Empire exhibition ticket is from 1924.

Initially working on his own, within two weeks two employees were taken on to keep up with demand.

Ernest Brook's sales strategy was to target the local mills and numerous small factories around Huddersfield who received their single phase electricity supply from the Huddersfield Corporation power station and invariably hired their motors from the same source. When Ernest Brook attempted to supply the Borough Council with his new motors, he was turned away by the Borough's Electrical Engineer, who was not convinced that the Brook motor was as reliable as the better known continental counterparts.

Armed with the belief that his motors were better than the competition, especially in their more efficient use of power and therefore running cost, it was decided to offer the Brook motor direct to the Corporation's customers at the same hiring rate plus 50% of the savings made in running costs. Almost all the customers were pleased with this bargain and quite quickly the Borough Electricity Department came into line.

So successful was this saving in running costs that the fame of the Brook motor spread to the surrounding manufacturing towns of the West Riding. By the end of his first year's trading, E. Brook employed eight staff and shortly afterwards became a limited company under the banner of E. Brook Ltd.

Above: A Christmas gathering in one of the Brook factories. Judging by the number of female employees and lack of men, this was taken towards the end of the war
Right: One of Brook's 1930s showvans, purpose built with interior wood panelling to be a mobile showroom for the company's motors and control gear.

The demand for electric motors began to grow rapidly and later in 1905 the firm moved to larger premises at Nelson Mill on Colne Road. Further expansion led to the opening of a showroom in Leeds and by 1912 Brooks had a London showroom and workshop. By 1914, just a decade after the firm began in one room on Threadneedle Street, E. Brook Ltd had agents in Birmingham, Glasgow, Cardiff, Bristol, Sheffield, Wakefield, Plymouth and abroad in New Zealand, Australia and Canada.

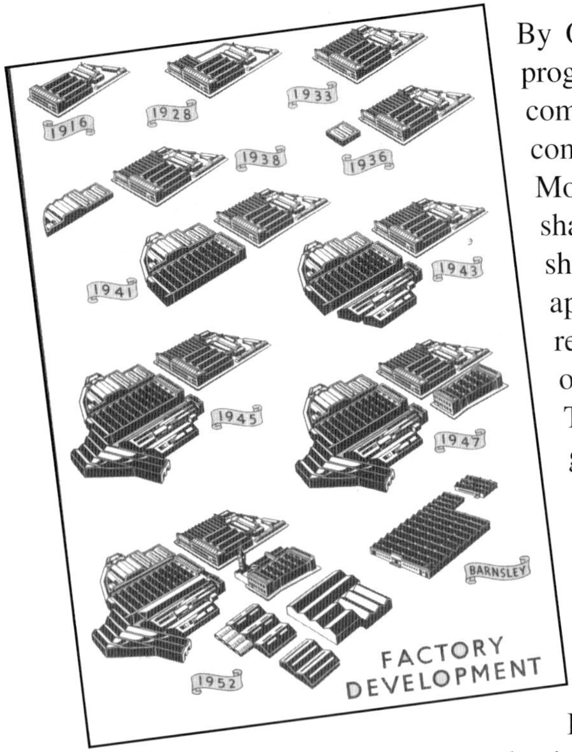

By October 1915 Brooks were continuing to make rapid progress and despite the onset of war, a new works were commissioned at Longroyd Bridge, taking two years to complete. The firm's title changed again in 1927 to Brook Motors Limited and the founder introduced his first profit sharing scheme, leading to many employees becoming shareholders in the company. By 1938 Brook employed approaching one thousand people and its founder relinquished the position of managing director, handing over to his two sons, Frank and Jack Brook.

Throughout the second world war the company made generators for airborne radar as well as air raid sirens and other motors for the general war effort.

During the 1950s and 60s the unabated expansion enjoyed by the company continued, with subsidiaries in the USA and Canada helping to boost the number of employees to a staggering 3,500, with one in three industrial electric motors in Britain made by Brooks.

By the late 1960s Brook Motors Limited, though still having its base and headquarters in Huddersfield, was a champion of international industry, winning the Queens award for exports in 1968. As a result of its achievements the business was acquired by Hawker Siddeley in 1970. Through mergers and acquisitions, the company was to become Brook Crompton Parkinson and was then bought out by one of Britain's top ten companies BTR in 1991. In 1993 the most up-to-date chapter of the firm began when the group was renamed Brook Hansen, incorporating the Brook Motors business and Hansen Transmission of Belgium. The Brook Hansen group created a company that is a world class manufacturer of motors, transmission gear and control units, thus encompassing the total drive requirements of its customers.

Visitors to Threadneedle Street in Huddersfield would be surprised to know that what started out as a one man business on a first floor room would become the global company that employs thousands of people on both sides of the Atlantic, including hundreds in Huddersfield.

Above: The speed at which Brook Motors grew in the early years was to have a profound effect on the surrounding buildings, as the company bought up or built on every piece of land as it became available. To give an idea of the rapid progress that the business made, in 1904 Brooks occupied 250 square feet of space, which had risen to 657,000 by 1957.

Right: The Empress Works were built in 1917 to the design decided by Ernest Brook. Opened by Mrs E. Brook, wife of the founder, a total of one thousand friends and employees attended the opening ceremony. The works were planned with the idea of providing easy progress of materials through the workshops with the least loss of time and labour and were initially used to supply motors for the war effort

Driving to Holme Moss in March 1953 was quite a challenge, as this picture shows. Looking at this bleak arctic scene, it's hard to believe that the winter of 1947 was much worse when this road was completely impassable. The snowfall in March 1963 is also said to be one of the worst on record. Strangely, the most severe winters have often been preceded by the hottest summers.

Left: Seen on Bradley Boulevard, Brackenhall, in May 1953 is the decorated Trolleybus which Huddersfield Corporation put into service for the duration of the Coronation celebrations of HM Queen Elizabeth II, who was crowned on the 2nd of June 1953. It was used on all the trolleybus routes on a rotational basis but didn't carry passengers. Although it was on duty on Coronation Day, few were out and about to see it driving through the streets, preferring instead to huddle in front of the few Television sets that were around at the time.

Right: Lord Street, from the early 1920s until 1974 when the new bus station was opened, was the starting point for destinations served by the Yorkshire Traction Co. This photograph was taken in 1964 and shows County Motors bus number 86, a Leyland Tiger PS2, new in December 1949. County Motors (Lepton) Ltd. was absorbed by Yorkshire Traction who now use the former County Garage at Waterloo as their operating base in Huddersfield.

Right: George Sykes and Company of Crosland Moor had a very well equipped and modern workshop, by the standards of the day when this picture was taken in 1962. It is strange to think that the cars assembled in this picture, including an Austin Healey Sprite, Austin A40 and no less than five "Aunty" Rovers, were just everyday cars then. Today these are all highly regarded as classic cars from an unforgettable era of British motoring.
Below right: Newton's Garage on the corner of Green Street and Viaduct Street, also in 1962. Newton's was remarkable in that it was the first garage in the area to offer a 24 hour filling station service. The attendant could be summoned in the small hours by ring a bell on the forecourt!
Below: Atkinsons, the main British Leyland dealer for Huddersfield in the early 1970s, was proudly announcing the arrival of the Austin 1300GT in this 1970 shot. The "GT that just had to be" was designed by Sir Alec Issigonis, the man behind two other post-war motoring icons, the Mini and the Morris Minor.

On Monday 13th February 1967 a Huddersfield Corporation trolleybus was involved in an unusual accident at the Dodlee terminus of the Longwood route. The driver misjudged the position of the trolleybus whilst reversing onto a platform which was built to allow vehicles to make three point turns at the terminus and return to town. The error caused the trolleybus to plunge 10 feet into the field alongside the platform and become wedged between an electricity sub-station and a stone wall. Recovery was a major operation involving the hire of a mobile crane, the use of ancillary vehicles from the transport department and the dismantling of the trolley lines overhead to allow the crane to lift the six year old trolleybus out of the field. It was later towed away for scrap. Interestingly, the bus involved -number 634- was one of the last ten trolleybuses to be purchased new by the Corporation in 1959.

Left: No prizes for guessing the year of this picture, taken outside Boyes Triumph Dealership in Queensgate. The newly launched Triumph 1300 was advertised at £796 12s 11d complete!

Below Left: Brockholes modern looking showroom in Westgate makes a sharp contrast to the older Victorian buildings further along the road. To the left of the Ford Popular is the car that was eventually to replace it in the Ford range, the Anglia.

Below: Over thirty shiny motors are pictured in this 1965 view of Boyes Garages used car showroom, including such marques as Standard, Morris and Singer. Perhaps the most profound aspect of this collection of sixties motorcars is that every single one of them was made in Britain!

'Here it is' proclaims the banner in Boyes' showroom window at Chapel Hill, circa 1960. The all new Triumph Herald Convertible was on sale to anyone wanting wind-in-the-hair and four seats, all for £766 2s 6d.

Below: Huddersfield Northern Union (Rugby League) Club 1913-14. Popularly known as the "team of all talents", the Huddersfield side of 1913-14 and 1914-15 is still widely recognised as one of the greatest ever to play the game. In 1913-14 they won the "Treble": The League Championship, the Challenge Cup and the Yorkshire League Cup with stars from all over the Empire. The Australian winger Albert Aaron Rosenfeld (fondly known as Rozzy) scored a remarkable 80 tries during the season - a record which still stands today and one which looks unlikely ever to be surpassed. Rosenfeld is seated on the left.

Right: Albert Aaron Rosenfeld - Tobacconists shop in 1915. The following year the "Fartowners" went one better and won all four competitions, adding the Yorkshire Cup to their previous seasons' haul. Their trophies were displayed in Rosenfeld's tobacconists shop next to the Empire cinema in John William Street. Seen with the trophies are: (Left to right) T. H. Grey, A. Bennett, and Albert A. Rosenfeld. The trophies are: (Left to right) The Yorkshire Challenge Cup, League Champions Cup and the Yorkshire League Cup. The frontage of the shop, now a newsagents, is still recognisable today.

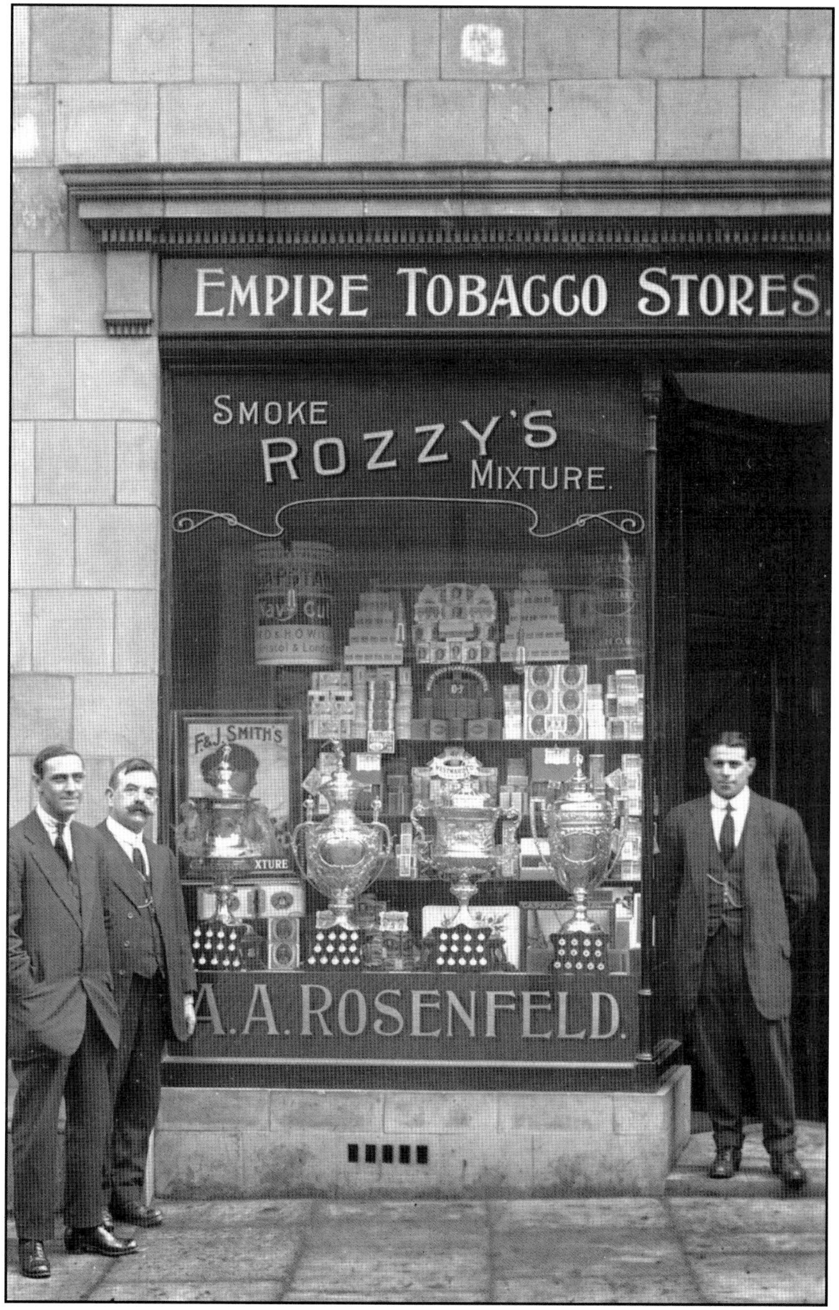

Huddersfield Rugby League Team in 1948-1949. Another great period in Fartown's history was the era spanning the late 1940s and early 1950s. This side won the championship play-off at Manchester City FC's Maine Road ground on Saturday May 14th 1949. Huddersfield beat Warrington 13-12 in an exciting match watched by the then World Record crowd for a Rugby League match of 75194 paying £11073 in receipts.

Huddersfield Town's Promotional squad 1952-53. After 32 years in Division 1, Town suffered its first relegation in 1952, but bounced straight back the following season with the above team gaining promotion. They set an all time Football League record when their defence (back row) went through the season unchanged. Back row: (left to right) L. Kelly, R. Staniforth, W. McGarry, J. Wheeler, L. Quested, D. McEvoy. Front row: A. Gunn, J. Watson, J. Glazzard, W. Davie, V. Metcalfe.

Right: Early sewing machines in operation at B. Crook's Huddersfield factory.

Above: The back page of one of Mitre's advertising brochures from the early sixties shows a young Denis Law sporting a Mitre tracksuit. Also available were "Stanley Matthews shinpads".

In 1817, Benjamin Crook started a small Leather tannery in Huddersfield. Nearly 200 years later, as Mitre Sports International Ltd., the same Company is known the world over for its sporting goods and footwear. A symbol of quality in sports equipment, its footballs are used wherever the game is played.

Mitre started using its expertise in leather for football and rugby in the 1880s when the games became established. Over the years, through acquisitions and expansions, Mitre has widened its activities to include the manufacture at various times of Squash, Badminton and Tennis Raquets, Billiard Tables, Golf Clubs and Fitness Equipment, besides Balls, Bags and Cricket equipment.

In the 1960s Grampian Holdings plc., a Scottish Group with a portfolio of Sports Companies, acquired Mitre and the subsequent expansion saw the Company add Sports footwear manufacturing to its other activities and begin to add an International dimension to its well-established home market.

In 1978, Mitre, was 'bursting out' of the premises it had occupied for more than 100 years and moved to larger ones nearby. This made possible the complete re-organisation of its manufacturing operations and transfer of all the footwear, accessories, cricket, soft leather bags, ball preparations and stitching operations, into one location.

Above: Circa. 1900, B. Crook and Son Ltd. workers are depicted sewing leather footballs together.

The re-organisation was completed without losing the unique core of expert craftsmen which assured Mitre's quality.

1981/82 saw Mitre in an unprecedented position in its home market. Ninety per-cent of English and one hundred per cent of Scottish Professional League Clubs played Mitre exclusively during that season and all four British cup finals, Scottish F.A., English League, English F.A. as well as all English, Scottish and Irish Internationals, were played with Mitre balls - a feat that had never been achieved before. This domination of the UK soccer scene continues until this day. Although Mitre has now been producing soccer balls for over hundred years they are not standing still with current materials and methods.

Mitre have a full-time development team on balls constantly investigating materials, construction, bounce, durability and flight characteristics. The launch of Mitre's distinctive Delta-designed ball in 1984 throughout the world has resulted in ever-increasing sales and presence of the Mitre brand. With this history and its current resources and expertise, Mitre looks forward to the future.

A remarkable story of achievement in Huddersfield.

Above: An early display showing the varied nature of leather sports goods produced at the time.

The partially completed new "West" stand with new tip-up seats, opened for the first time on 23rd September 1950 for the visit of Sheffield Wednesday in a First Division Fixture. The original stand had been gutted by fire in the previous April and Town were compelled to play two of their remaining "Home"fixures at Elland Road, Leeds. The fire, which started in a small corner stand next to the houses on Leeds Road (which are still standing and are evident in the photograph) spread rapidly in a strong Northerly wind. Within minutes the whole stand, which ran the length of the touchline, was ablaze. Luckily, it was Thursday afternoon and a few office staff inside were quickly and safely evacuated.

Huddersfield Town's Promotional squad 1969-70. After 14 years in the backwaters of Division 2, Huddersfield Town finally won promotion back to the top flight of English Football - Division 1 as it was then - by clinching the championship. Pictured at the training ground on Leeds Road Playing Fields are: Back row (left to right) D. Shaw, R. Mielczarek, F. Worthington, R. Ellam, D. Lawson, T. Poole, T. Cherry, P. Aimson, B. Greenhalgh. Front Row: C. Dobson, S. Smith, J. Lawson, J. McGill, J. Nicholson, G. Hutt, R. Hoy, D. Clarke.

The changing face of the town centre

Buxton Road in August 1956. This area was demolished in the late 1960s and the "Hammerson" development erected in its place, housing the C&A Store. By the 1970s, the name Buxton Road had been dropped in favour of New Street. The Curzon Cinema, formerly the Picturedome, was a popular venue, as was the snack bar next door. Closer inspection of this street scene reveals the presence of the early TV sets in the windows of H. Wigfall and Son as well as in the van outside the shop.

New Street in January 1953. Long before yellow lines made their appearance, the traffic on New Street could be quite heavy. A bread van is on the left of this bustling scene with freshly baked loaves on racks waiting to be unloaded.

Above: Huddersfield Parish Church taken in July 1950. The area in front of the church was used as a bus terminus for many years.

Left: Built in 1881, this fine Italianate building on the corner of Cloth Hall Street, pictured here in 1965, housed the Midland Bank. Its controversial replacement was commissioned in 1971. The dome of the building was a distinctive part of the landscape of Huddersfield town centre and can be seen in many of the town centre views in the pages of this book.

Left: St. George's Square, Huddersfield in September 1953. The railway station was built between 1846 and 1850 for the Huddersfield and Manchester (later London and North Western) and Lancashire and Yorkshire Railways. The central part of the building was initially built as an hotel. Four years prior to this photograph, the statue of Sir Robert Peel was removed from St. George's Square where it had been since 1873.

Right: This 1962 photograph is dominated by High Street Buildings on the corner of High Street and Buxton Road (since renamed New Street) . Built in 1935, High Street Buildings have survived to this day, but the rest of the shops and buildings further along Buxton Road were flattened to make way for the Hammerson development.

Left: King Street in 1957. Pictured is Wallaces Ltd. Grocery and Provisions store with the Kingsway Cafe above it. The Cafe served luncheons, teas and suppers. In Wallace's windows, Nescafe was on special offer at the time at 2s 9d per tin.

Below left: Huddersfield has seen two department stores come and go, Rushworths on John William Street and Heywoods based at Market Street, pictured here in this photograph from July 1969.

Below: This is a view of Cloth Hall Street taken in March 1954. The ABC/Ritz Cinema and Restaurant on Market street is clearly visible. The Volkswagen Beetle with split rear window would have been one of the rare foreign cars on Huddersfield's streets at the time.

Right: Devonshire Buildings, better known as Boots Corner, at the junction of King Street and Victoria Lane in September 1950. Next up from Boots was one of Montague Burton's Shops - "The Tailor of Taste".

Below: New Street in 1962. Closer inspection reveals that the three shoe shops next to each other on New Street are stocked with the ladies fashion favourite of the time, the stiletto heeled shoe. Some dance halls later introduced "stiletto bans" after the offending shoes left polished wooden floors with thousands of small indentations.

Westgate, looking down towards Burtons at the junction of John William Street and Market Place. This photograph, taken on a hot summer's day in July 1950, clearly shows the trolley lines snaking down the middle of the road.

Also taken in July 1950, this view of New Street captures the atmosphere of the era. The traffic lights in the foreground mark out the junction of High Street, New Street, Buxton Road and Ramsden Street. The Police Constable on the right would be looking out for motorists 'jumping' red lights. Judging by the pair of white gloves in his hand , he may have been about to go on point duty, directing traffic. Further down New Street a Bentley & Shaws Ltd lorry can be seen delivering barrels of Town Bitter, the local brew. The ornate dome of the Midland Bank building is also visible at the end of New Street, as in the light coloured store of the Burtons Building.

Possibly one of the most recognisable scenes in this book, the Market Place, taken in 1962. The headlines on the "Empire News" billboards announce a 'Big Yorkshire Garage Blaze". During 1962, other national headlines included: Marilyn Monroe's suicide, Denis Law becoming the first £100,000 footballer when he transferred from Turin to Manchester United and the last London Smog occurred, killing 28 people. The resulting Clean Air Act had a profound impact on the mill chimneys around Huddersfield.

Right: D' Agostino's Ice Cream Parlour in the Market Hall taken during 1960.

Bottom Right: This 1966 scene shows King Street and an exterior view of the Market Hall. Judging by the number of vans loading and the Market Hall Clock, this was an early morning picture. A great many people were saddened by the closure of the "old" Market Hall on March 28th 1970, prior to the opening of the new Market Hall three days later.

Below: The Co-op building on Buxton Road, shown in this early January picture taken circa 1961. The main building dates from the end of the last century with the new section on the right of the picture being completed in 1936. 1961 was the year that the first traffic wardens were introduced to Britain and the yellow lines would be present outside the Co-op not many years later.

Left: Taken from the rooftops of the Gas Showrooms, this wide angle view of the buildings off High Street was taken in 1957.
This whole block was demolished to make way for the building of the Civic centre (phase one) in the early sixties.

Right: Civic Centre phase 1 under construction, built by local builders Wimpenny & Co. of Linthwaite. Part of Manchester Street Bus Station is seen in the bottom left of the picture. This was built in 1948. At the centre left hand side of this view is the George and Dragon Pub which called last orders for the final time in 1964 when Manchester Street closed to traffic.
Behind the George and Dragon can be seen the two office blocks built around 1957. The block on the right being the Gas Showroom on the site of the Methodist Chapel closed during World War Two. The Gas Showrooms were operated by the North East Gas Board and replaced the old municiple Gas Showrooms in Byram Street

Right: In 1968 major building work was underway in the area surrounding the Library. The area shown in this photograph was formerly occupied by the Theatre Royal which was one of the casualties of the redevelopment, as were the buildings off Ramsden Street, formerly housing many Local Government departments. The library itself survived intact. It had been completed in 1940 by local builders Wimpenny & Co. Ltd, and the basement had been used as a First Aid post during World War Two.

Left: 1960 saw the building of the new Telephone Exchange progressing rapidly. This was the beginning of the decade that saw a great deal of development in Huddersfield and a tower block can be seen rising in the background. The Southgate Hotel was knocked down to accommodate the Telephone Exchange within a few months of this picture being taken.

May 1968 and the Town Centre redevelopment plan was well underway, as this picture shows. The quagmire that this building site had become was where the Police and Fire stations had been, prior to their demolition The new Market Hall was to be built on this site, opening its doors for the first time on March 31st 1970. In the distance building work can be seen progressing on the Buxton House tower block, behind what was then Buxton Road, later to be renamed New Street. This part of the town centre redevelopment was known as "phase two", with the Civic Centre, Police Station and magistrates Court representing phase one.

This damp day in March 1971 saw a great deal of activity on the site of the new Boots store on Victoria Lane. The site had formerly been occupied by the Market Hall , which had closed its doors for the last time just a year before this picture was taken. Most of the redevelopment of the Town Centre area had been completed by the end of the 60s, including The Piazza shopping precinct, new Market Hall and the Hammerson development on what was formerly Buxton Road. Like many other towns, Huddersfield's architecture was to see many changes in the 60s, when the availability of money and new town planning ideas resulted in a wave of redevelopment across the country.

One of Slaithwaite's best known pubs, the Star Hotel is actually in Linthwaite, the boundary between Slaithwaite and Linthwaite being the stream running under the bridge in the foreground, the bus stop is actually along the boundary. Town Ales were brewed by Bentley and Shaw Ltd at Lockwood Brewery. In 1948 they were taken over by Hammonds and later Charringtons absorbed Hammonds. The Star Garage is seen selling premium grade petrol at 1s 5d per gallon - 7p at today's values. The photograph is believed to have been taken in the summer of 1937, the clues being the overhead wiring erected during the summer and autumn of 1937 for the impending conversions from trams to trolleybuses which took place on April 10 1938. This road, the A62T, was one of the primary trunk roads linking Yorkshire with Lancashire. After the M62 was opened the road lost its Trunk route status.

Three street scenes of Kirkburton taken in the late summer of 1952. On the surface, parts of Kirkburton, which was mentioned in the Doomsday Book, appear relatively unchanged to this day. Closer inspection reveals significant improvements to everything concerned with transport in the photographs; the slippery cobbled roads were poorly lit at this time, the quality of the brakes and steering of the vehicles pictured were a far cry from those of today's modern machines, and even butchers have made what some would call *progress* in the field of transportation!

These three photographs really capture the atmosphere of the early fifties - less than a decade after the end of the Second World War when life was returning to relative stability.

New Hey Road was constructed under the Turnpike Road Acts in the 1830s to link New Hey between Oldham and Rochdale with Huddersfield. The two chimneys just visible belong to P. Martin and Sons' Wellington Mills , Oakes who were renowned for their fine worsted and Ben Crossland Oakes Mill who manufactured woollen cloths. This photograph was taken in the summer of 1938 . The semi-detached houses were built between 1936 and 1938 by local builders, Wadsworths, and sold for £500 or £520 if a single gararge was included. The motorcar BCX23 was registered new in March 1938.

July 26th 1949, saw a Royal visit to Huddersfield, when Princess Elizabeth and the Duke of Edinburgh came to the town. This photograph, taken from a second floor window on New Street, shows the Royal motorcade moving towards Market Place. The size of the crowds on New Street is simply amazing. In order to gain a better view some onlookers can be seen on the roof of the Fifty Shilling Tailors, and staff at the Midland Bank on the Corner of Cloth Hall Street made good use of the stone balcony.

The pictures on this and the next page were all taken on the day of the Royal visit to Huddersfield in July 1949.

Left: The Royal party leave Learoyd Brothers & Co. on Leeds Road. To the right of Princess Elizabeth is Alderman D. Cartwright, who was Mayor at the time. Alderman Cartwright's daughter Shirley Cartwright is next to Prince Philip. The expressions of excitement on the faces of the factory girls reflects the magnitude of the occasion; Royal visits really were major events in the days before television coverage made Royal faces and activities as familiar as they are today.

Right: Pupils of Waverly School, Edgerton road, wave to the Royal car as it approaches Huddersfield. Fortunately, the weather on the day was glorious, as this picture shows.

Right: Bunting and flags of the Commonwealth are much in evidence in this view of the Imperial Arcade photographed in May 1953, shortly before the Coronation of Queen Elizabeth the Second.

Below: Staff from the ICI works on Leeds Road had their own message for Princess Elizabeth on her visit in 1949, presumably relating to Prince Charles.

Left: Rushworths department store on John William Street, fully decked out in Coronation decorations, as were most of the shops in the town centre during May 1953. Many people would say that the popularity of television really took off after the Coronation, with people gathering round the small number of sets available.

Below, left: Not quite as extravagant, but even small villages like Holmfirth, shown here in May 1953, were well decorated.

Below: The railway station also benefitted from Coronation decorations to its frontage - as did most civic and public buildings around the Country. The stonework as shown on this picture appears very blackened compared to the warmer stone hues of today - one of the benefits of the Clean Air Acts.

Left: The Guard of Honour march past the Fire Station in the aptly named Princess Street, while the Royal couple visited the Town Hall during their visit of July 1949.

Right: On the steps of the Town Hall, Princess Elizabeth is shown standing next to Alderman Cartwright and his daughter Shirley, whilst the Huddersfied Labour MP at the time, JPW Mallieu stands at the rear of the party, in front of the Town Clerk, Harry Brown, seen wearing his ceremonial wig.

Right: The Royal Couple leave the Town in an open topped car at the finale of their visit in 1949, with large crowds lining the route.

Below: The crowds in Byram Street were certainly gathering for a Royal visit but on this occasion it was Princess Margaret's turn to visit Huddersfield Parish Church in April 1953. There was much to celebrate in that particular year, with the Coronation of Queen Elizabeth and the climbing of Mount Everest by Sir Edmund Hillary and Sherpa Tensing hitting the headlines on the same day.

The development taking place around Buxton Road (later renamed New Street) is clearly visible in this aerial photograph circa 1968. Work is well underway in the area of the Law Courts and the "new" Police Station, whilst the Civic Centre appears to be at a late stage of its construction work. The Civic Centre opened its doors on October 1st 1965, with the Magistrates Courts opening in February 1968.

Shore Head Roundabout dominates this aerial photograph, also taken in 1965. This view looking from the South Eastern end of town provides a good opportunity to see the 'old' Market Hall on King Street with its glass roof panels. The roof of the former Hippodrome Theatre is visible on the left of the picture. The Hippodrome became the Tudor Cinema in 1930 later changing its name again to Essoldos before falling victim to a fire in 1967.

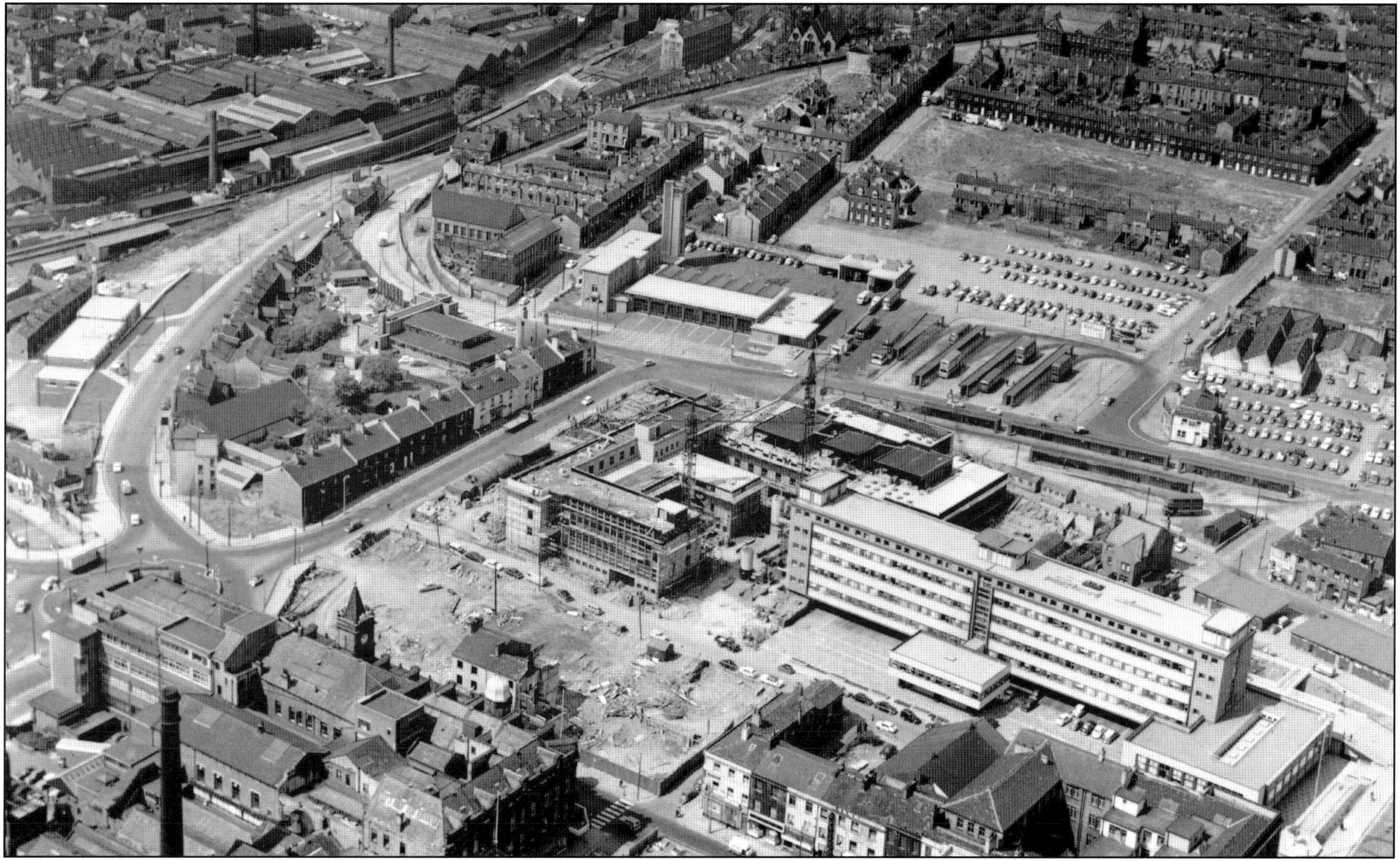

Another view of the Civic Centre/ Magistrates Court and "new" Police Station in 1965 with the Upper Head Row Bus Station visible behind. The "new" Fire Station, adjacent to the Bus Station, can also be seen. Demolition work is underway on the buildings at the north side of Buxton Road which would lead to the building of the C & A Store and Buxton House during the two years after this photograph was taken. The Curzon Cinema can just be seen in the bottom of this picture on Buxton Road. Sadly it was also soon to be flattened.

The lower half of this 1965 aerial view is dominated by the modern looking buildings of Huddersfield Polytechnic (later to be granted University status). The Police station and local government offices on Ramsden Street are all intact in this photograph, but would be demolished before the end of the 1960s to make way for the new Market Hall. The old Market Hall, visible in the top centre of this shot, closed its doors on March 31st 1970 and was then pulled down, much to the dismay of a great many local people.

Armitages, serving Huddersfield's gardeners for generations.

William Armitage, 1808-1876, founder of Armitages.

Nowadays, Armitages Garden Centres are well known as part of Huddersfield's thriving business community, serving their customers from their centres at Birchencliffe and Shelley. Perhaps less well known is the fact that the company began over 150 years ago, making it one of Huddersfield's longest established businesses.

Armitages began in 1842 when William Armitage set up his corn and seed warehouse in the town's Beast Market. Some years later, the business moved to number four New Street (later re-numbered number seven), which was to be the home of Armitages for over one hundred years.

William died in 1910, with the business transferring to his sons. Armitages traded from number four New Street for many years, surviving the difficulties that two world wars brought. In the period following the Second World War, business grew and the company did well from its New street premises, which by now represented a prime site on the busiest streets in Huddersfield.

By 1963 Armitages had reached the stage where the New Street shop was no longer big enough to hold the stocks of seeds and gardening equipment that Armitages were now renowned for. The remedy for this was to move to larger premises, and so Armitages relocated to number one, Lord Street.

The new, larger premises at Lord Street enabled Armitages to expand into garden furniture and machinery, which became the responsibility of Quinton Armitage. Soon after a garden machinery repair service was offered, with the basement of Lord Street acting as the workshop, before separate premises were acquired in the Beast Market. In 1976 the garden machinery side was again expanded into new premises on Old Leeds Road, housing both a showroom and workshop.

Eleven years later, in 1985, the Pennine Garden Centre was opened, followed by the Mower Centre and Garden Centre at Birchencliffe in 1991 that replaced the two town centre operations. In 1992 Armitages celebrated a century and a half of service to Hudersfield's gardeners. The business is still owned and run by the Armitage family, who look forward to the next 150 years with confidence.

Left: Bell Armitage, son of the founder, William, with his wife Elizabeth and daughter in the grounds of the family home at Rowley Grove, Fenay Bridge. ***Above:*** a 1958 seed catalogue, showing the New Street shop.

Lawrence Batley, the Huddersfield man who founded the Cash and Carry Industry

For almost 40 years, Huddersfield-based Batleys have been synonymous with all that's best in cash & carry. And with good reason - because chairman, Lawrence Batley is widely recognised as the founder of the industry in this country. Back in 1958, at a time when other wholesalers were working on average margins of 10 per cent, he made his mark by cutting his to two-and-a-half per cent and asking customers to collect their own goods.

Based in a former laundry - boasting a leaky roof that necessitated many of the items on display having to be covered in sacking - Mr Batley ordered the goods, sold them and even did the book-keeping. Takings were kept in an old Oxo tin, secured by a rubber band. Things were tough, but the business was revolutionised overnight when he was persuaded to buy a cash register. However, Mr Batley was not without his opponents.

Several of Huddersfield's larger traders of the time began circulating rumours that he was going bankrupt and certain rival wholesalers even met to try and stop supplies being delivered to Batleys.

Despite such negative opposition, the major manufacturers continued to support him and the fledgling firm carried on. Never one to shirk a challenge, Mr Batley armed himself with promotional leaflets and personally slogged around the town informing his customers that everything was in good shape. But the campaign took its toll and left him in poor health - weighing only six-and-a-half stones and suffering from ulcers and asthma.

Always convinced that he would succeed though, Mr Batley dug deep and bounced back. The rest, as they say, is history and today the company he began operate 14 depots from Birmingham and Coventry to Edinburgh and Glasgow. Each offers an average of 20,000 different lines, including an extensive selection of own-label beers, wines & spirits, catering and grocery products. Birmingham, Doncaster, Glasgow, Manchester and Newcastle also boast separate pet food warehouses, which will soon be joined by others at Bradford, Coventry and Preston. From the outset, the company have been firmly behind the independent retailer and caterer and operate a strict trade-only policy.

Where it all began - Sheepridge, Huddersfield in 1957.

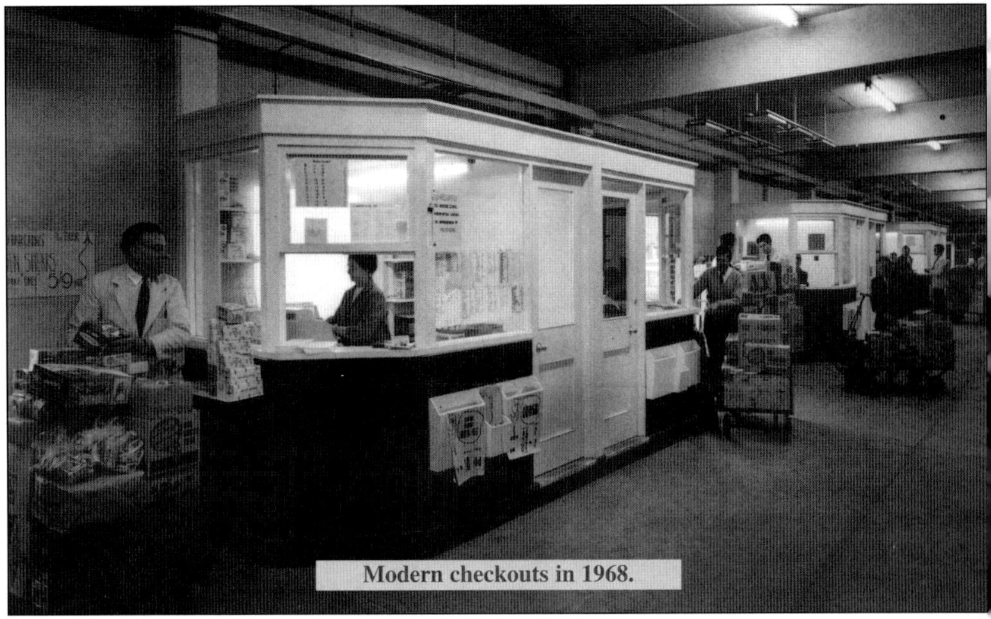

Modern checkouts in 1968.

In the early days it was real pioneering stuff - with Mr Batley writing orders on a cigarette packet while perched on an upturned orange box quite a common site at his first depot, a former Huddersfield laundry. That's a far cry from today's sophisticated operation, with Batleys recently claiming to be the first national cash & carry operator to fully install laser-scanning at the checkouts. But despite this and many other technological advances one thing has remained constant: giving customers a fast, efficient service backed by a competitive pricing structure. Such qualities are very much a Batleys hallmark.

The company's motto: 'The first - and still the best' is something they derive great pride from. It runs alongside a policy of: 'small profits make for a large turnover', reflecting their determination to help independent retailers and corner shop owners compete effectively against the supermarkets.

At the end of his first financial year, Mr Batley was doubtless delighted with his turnover of £15,000. Today, the business he began generates annual sales of around half-a-billion pounds, with profits approaching six million.

In the interim, Mr Batley admits to receiving several offers to buy the company, including one from Tesco, but says that he never had any intention of selling. Indeed, the business was brought back into private ownership by the Batley family in 1990. Today they employ more than 1,300 staff and are now actively seeking to expand even further down than the Midlands and into the South of England.

Grosvenor Chemicals Limited

Whyte Chemical Group of Companies

CHEMICAL MANUFACTURERS

TOLL SYNTHESIS

FORMULATION SERVICES

Grosvenor Works, Linthwaite,
Huddersfield, West Yorkshire
HD7 5QL

Telephone 01484 842451

Facsimile 01484 847066

Jarmain

Wool technology at its best

George Jarmain was a well known chemistry teacher at the King James School in Almondbury. He subsequently became the Huddersfield Borough Analyst and developed the Carbonising process in response after a plea from local textile manufacturers to find a method to recover the wool content from wool/cotton waste. In 1873, he and his son founded Jarmain and Son Limited to commercialise this process. The company was originally on the site of what is today the ICI Plant, and in 1898 moved to the present Minerva Works site.

The Company remained in family ownership until 1969, and in 1978 (under Berisford International ownership) Kirkheaton became the focal point of their plan to rationalise the group's wool processing activity.

In December 1990 the company joined the textile group Illingworth, Morris Limited and during the following period the business of Alston Scouring Company was transferred to the Kirkheaton site.

The Company's main activities now are Scouring, Carbonising, Kroy Shrink- resist process, and speciality chemical treatment of wool.

Jarmain and Son Limited,
Minerva Works,
Kirkheaton, Huddersfield, West
Yorkshire
HD5 0QP.
Tel 01484 549011
Fax 01484 536680

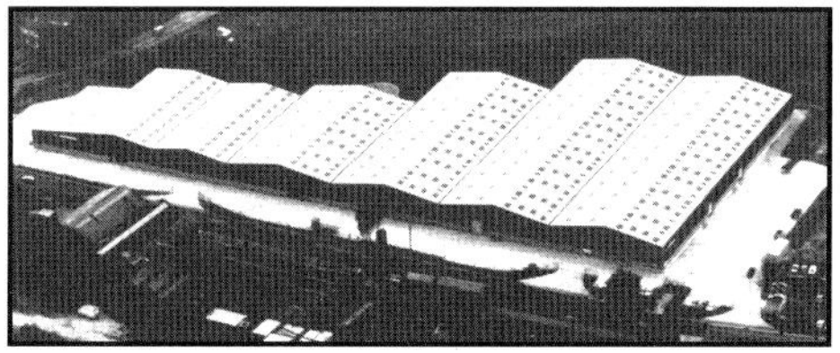

Jarmain
Commission Wool Processors

GREENHEAD BOOKS

Briers
HAIR STYLISTS
REMINGTON